A Glimpse of Glory

Studies on Christian Character

Max Lucado

General Editor

A GLIMPSE OF GLORY
STUDIES ON CHRISTIAN CHARACTER

Cover Art by Koechel Peterson and Associates, Inc., Minneapolis, Minnesota. Interior design and composition by Design Corps, Batavia, IL.

Produced with the assistance of the Livingstone Corporation. Study questions written by Christopher Hudson, Carol Smith, and Valerie Weidemann.

ISBN 0-8499-5427-4

Contents

Introduction

The cheering crowds at the stadium fade away. The plaques on the wall end up in someone's attic. Awards and honors eventually diminish. Fame wanes and popularity declines.

The applause of earth is all-too predictable in its temporariness.

But though the world's recognition is tentative, heaven's applause is forever. It is a joy that only God can give. It is knowing that the God who created you, who crafted a self-sacrificing plan to save you, looks upon you with a sacred delight. A holy gladness. And, because he loves you, he wants to share that same joy with you. It's an unmistakable peek into a holy realm: a glimpse of glory.

—Max Lucado

Sacred Delight

"What is sacred delight? It is God doing what gods would be doing only in your wildest dreams—wearing diapers, riding donkeys, washing feet, dozing in storms."

—Max Lucado

1

1. What does "sacred delight" mean to you?

_____

_____

_____

_____

_____

_____

_____

_____

A Moment with Max

Max shares these insights with us in his book *The Applause of Heaven*.

Sacred delight is good news coming through the back door of your heart. It's what you'd always dreamed but never expected. It's the too-good-to-be-true coming true. It's having God as your pinch-hitter, your lawyer, your dad, your biggest fan, and your best friend. God on your side, in your heart, out in front, and protecting your back. It's hope where you least expect it— a flower in life's sidewalk.

It is sacred because only God can grant it. It is a delight because it thrills. Since it is sacred, it can't be stolen. And since it is delightful, it can't be predicted.

It was this gladness that danced through the Red Sea. It was this joy that blew the trumpet at Jericho. It was this secret that made Mary sing. It was this surprise that put the springtime into Easter morning. It is God's gladness. It's sacred delight.

And it is this sacred delight that Jesus promises in the Sermon on the Mount.

Nine times he promises it. And he promises it to an unlikely crowd.

2. How does it make you feel to know that God is your pinch-hitter?

_____

_____

_____

_____

3. Why do you think Jesus opened the Sermon on the Mount by talking about happiness?

_____

_____

_____

_____

A Message from the Word

³ "Those people who know they have great spiritual needs are happy,
  because the kingdom of heaven belongs to them.
⁴ Those who are sad now are happy,
  because God will comfort them.
⁵ Those who are humble are happy,
  because the earth will belong to them.
⁶ Those who want to do right more than anything else are happy,
  because God will fully satisfy them.
⁷ Those who show mercy to others are happy,
  because God will show mercy to them.
⁸ Those who are pure in their thinking are happy,
  because they will be with God.
⁹ Those who work to bring peace are happy,
  because God will call them his children.
¹⁰ Those who are treated badly for doing good are happy,
  because the kingdom of heaven belongs to them.

Matthew 5:3-10

4. How does Jesus' definition of happiness differ from our society's perspective?

3

_____

_____

_____

_____

_____

5. In which of the circumstances listed in this passage do you think it would be most difficult to feel happy?

_____

_____

_____

_____

6. List some ways that God's view of happiness challenges our own.

_____

_____

_____

_____

_____

More from the Word

⁶ My share in life has been pleasant;
     my part has been beautiful.
⁷ I praise the Lord because he advises me.
    Even at night, I feel his leading.
⁸ I keep the Lord before me always.
    Because he is close by my side,
      I will not be hurt.
⁹ So I rejoice and am glad.
    Even my body has hope,
¹⁰ because you will not leave me in the grave.
    You will not let your holy one rot.
¹¹ You will teach me how to live a holy life.
    Being with you will fill me with joy;
      at your right hand I will find pleasure forever.

Psalm 16:6-11

7. Why do we sometimes feel abandoned, despite God's promise that he will never leave us?

_____

_____

_____

_____

_____

8. How does God's presence bring us joy and hope in the midst of life's struggles?

_____

_____

_____

_____

_____

9. Describe a time when you felt joy, even though your circumstances were less than ideal.

_____

_____

_____

_____

_____

My Reflections

"There is a delicious gladness that comes from God. A holy joy. A sacred delight.

"And it is within your reach. You are one decision away from joy...

"But this joy is not cheap. What Jesus promises is not a gimmick to give you goose bumps nor a mental attitude that has to be pumped up at pep rallies. No, Matthew 5 describes God's radical reconstruction of the heart."

—Max

Journal

What steps can I take to become more aware of the joy God promises?

For Further Study

To study more about joy and happiness, read Psalm 1:1-3; Proverbs 8:34-36; Romans 4:7-8; Ephesians 3:14-21; James 1:12.

Additional Questions

10. What things keep us from experiencing the joy God has for us?

_____

_____

_____

_____

_____

_____

11. What personal sacrifices do we need to make in order to experience true joy?

_____

_____

_____

_____

_____

_____

12. How do you think others are affected when they see believers displaying joy and peace in difficult circumstances?

_____

_____

_____

_____

_____

_____

Additional Thoughts

_____

_____

9

_____

_____

_____

_____

_____

_____

_____

_____

_____

_____

_____

10

The Summit

"Before [Jesus] went to the masses, he went to the mountain. Before the disciples encountered the crowds, they encountered the Christ. And before they faced the people, they were reminded of the sacred."—Max Lucado

1. In what kinds of places do you feel closest to God?

_____

_____

_____

_____

_____

_____

_____

_____

_____

A Moment with Max

Max shares these insights with us in his book *The Applause of Heaven*.

You've been there. You've escaped the sandy foundations of the valley and ascended his grand outcropping of granite. You've turned your back on the noise and sought his voice. You've stepped away from the masses and followed the Master as he led you up the winding path to the summit.

His summit. Clean air. Clear view. Crisp breeze. The roar of the marketplace is down there, and the perspective of the peak is up here.

I read recently about a man who had breathed the summit air. His trips up the trail began early in his life and sustained him to the end. A few days before he died, a priest went to visit him in the hospital. As the priest entered the room, he noticed an empty chair beside the man's bed. The priest asked him if someone had been by to visit. The old man smiled, "I place Jesus on that chair, and I talk to him."

The priest was puzzled, so the man explained. "Years ago a friend told me that prayer was as simple as talking to a good friend. So every day I pull up a chair, invite Jesus to sit, and we have a good talk."

Some days later, the daughter of this man came to the parish house to inform the priest that her father had just died. "Because he seemed so content," she said, "I left him in his room alone for a couple of hours. When I got back to the room, I found him dead. I noticed a strange thing, though: His head was resting, not on the pillow, but on an empty chair that was beside his bed."

Learn a lesson from the man with the chair.

2. Describe a mountain top experience in your spiritual life.

_____

_____

_____

_____

_____

3. What helps you feel God's presence in your everyday life?

_____

_____

_____

_____

_____

A Message from the Word

⁴ I ask only one thing from the Lord.
   This is what I want:
   Let me live in the Lord's house
      all my life.
   Let me see the Lord's beauty
      and look with my own eyes at his Temple.
⁵ During danger he will keep me safe in his shelter.
   He will hide me in his Holy Tent,
      or he will keep me safe on a high mountain.
⁶ My head is higher than my enemies around me.
   I will offer joyful sacrifices in his Holy Tent.
      I will sing and praise the Lord.
⁷ Lord, hear me when I call;
   have mercy and answer me.
⁸ My heart said of you, "Go, worship him."
   So I come to worship you, Lord.

Psalm 27:4-8

4. What things keep us from spending time with God?

_____

_____

_____

_____

_____

5. List some ways we can seek God.

_____

_____

_____

_____

_____

6. What do we gain from worshiping God privately?

_____

_____

_____

_____

More from the Word

35 Early the next morning, while it was still dark, Jesus woke and left the house. He went to a lonely place, where he prayed.

Mark 1:35

16 Jesus traveled to Nazareth, where he had grown up. On the Sabbath day he went to the synagogue, as he always did, and stood up to read.

Luke 4:16

7. What does it tell us about Jesus that it was his custom to go to the synagogue?

_____

_____

_____

_____

_____

8. How do you imagine Jesus' disciples would describe his prayer life?

_____

_____

_____

_____

_____

_____

9. Why do you think Jesus chose to consistently spend time alone *with* God, even though he *was* God?

_____

_____

_____

_____

_____

_____

My Reflections

"Learn a lesson from the man with the chair . . . Take a trip with the King to the mountain peak. It's pristine, uncrowded, and on top of the world. Stubborn joy begins by breathing deep up there before you go crazy down here."—Max

Journal

How can I overcome the barriers that keep me from spending time with God?

_____

_____

_____

_____

_____

_____

_____

_____

_____

_____

_____

_____

_____

_____

_____

_____

17

For Further Study

To study more about spending time with God, read Deuteronomy 4:29; Psalm 46:8-11;105:1-4; Luke 4:14-16; Jude 1:20-21.

Additional Questions

10. What do we miss when we neglect our time alone with God?

_____

_____

_____

_____

_____

_____

_____

11. How would you describe what it means to "be still" before God?

_____

_____

_____

_____

_____

12. Has spending time in God's presence changed you? Explain.

_____

_____

_____

_____

_____

_____

Additional Thoughts

_____

_____

19

_____

_____

_____

_____

_____

_____

_____

_____

_____

_____

The Affluent Poor

"*You don't impress the officials at NASA with a paper airplane. You don't boast about your crayon sketches in the presence of Picasso. You don't claim equality with Einstein because you can write 'H$_2$O.' And you don't boast about your goodness in the presence of the Perfect.*"
                    —*Max Lucado*

1. If we lived in a universe where God's goodness was considered wealth, how would we become rich?

_____

_____

_____

_____

_____

_____

_____

A Moment with Max

Max shares these insights with us in his book *The Applause of Heaven.*

The first step to joy is a plea for help, an acknowledgment of moral destitution, an admission of inward paucity. Those who taste God's presence have declared spiritual bankruptcy and are aware of their spiritual crisis. Their cupboards are bare. Their pockets are empty. Their options are gone. They have long since stopped demanding justice; they are pleading for mercy.

They don't brag; they beg.

They ask God to do for them what they can't do without him. They have seen how holy God is and how sinful they are and have agreed with Jesus' statement, "Salvation is impossible."

Oh, the irony of God's delight—born in the parched soil of destitution rather than the fertile ground of achievement.

It's a different path, a path we're not accustomed to taking. We don't often declare our impotence. Admission of failure is not usually admission into joy. Complete confession is not commonly followed by total pardon. But then again, God has never been governed by what is common.

2. How can admitting helplessness lead to joy and freedom?

22

_____

_____

_____

_____

_____

3. What keeps people from admitting their need for God?

_____

_____

_____

_____

_____

A Message from the Word

[7] So that I would not become too proud of the wonderful things that were shown to me, a painful physical problem was given to me. This problem was a messenger from Satan, sent to beat me and keep me from being too proud. [8] I begged the Lord three times to take this problem away from me. [9] But he said to me, "My grace is enough for you. When you are weak, my power is made perfect in you." So I am very happy to brag about my weaknesses. Then Christ's power can live in me. [10] For this reason I am happy when I have weaknesses, insults, hard times, sufferings, and all kinds of troubles for Christ. Because when I am weak, then I am truly strong.

2 Corinthians 12:7-10

4. How does the grace of God affect the way we view our own frailties?

_____

_____

_____

_____

23

_____

_____

5. When have you seen the power of God shine through someone's weaknesses?

_____

_____

_____

_____

_____

_____

_____

6. How does knowing that God works through your weaknesses affect the way you feel about your failures?

_____

_____

_____

_____

_____

_____

More from the Word

24   ¹⁷ Command those who are rich with things of this world not to be proud. Tell them to hope in God, not in their uncertain riches. God richly gives us everything to enjoy. ¹⁸ Tell the rich people to do good, to be rich in doing good deeds, to be generous and ready to share. ¹⁹ By doing that, they will be saving a treasure for themselves as a strong foundation for the future. Then they will be able to have the life that is true life.

1 Timothy 6:17–19

7. In your own words, how would you describe true life?

_____

_____

_____

_____

_____

8. Why is it difficult for wealthy people to put their hope in God?

_____

_____

_____

_____

_____

_____

9. According to this passage, how can you build a strong foundation for your future?

_____

_____

_____

_____

My Reflections

"Mark it down. God does not save us because of what we've done. Only a puny god could be bought with tithes. Only an egotistical god would be impressed with our pain. Only a temperamental god could be satisfied by sacrifices. Only a heartless god would sell salvation to the highest bidders.

"And only a great God does for his children what they can't do for themselves."

—Max

Journal

I need you God because ...

_____

_____

_____

_____

_____

_____

_____

_____

_____

_____

_____

_____

_____

_____

_____

_____

_____

_____

For Further Study

To study more about your need for God, read Psalm 116:1-7; Romans 8:24-27; 1 Corinthians 1:25-31.

Additional Questions

10. What is spiritual wealth?

_____

_____

_____

_____

_____

_____

11. How does pride separate us from God?

_____

_____

_____

_____

_____

_____

_____

12. In what tangible ways can we demonstrate that our hope is in God, not in our riches?

_____

_____

_____

_____

_____

_____

_____

Additional Thoughts

_____

_____

_____

_____

_____

_____

_____

_____

_____

_____

_____

_____

The Broken Hearted

"Of all the paths to joy, this one has to be the strangest. True blessedness, Jesus says, begins with deep sadness. 'Blessed are those who know they are in trouble and have enough sense to admit it.' " —Max Lucado

1. Think of a time that you really regretted something you had done. If you could compare those feelings to a color palette, what colors would it include?

_____

_____

_____

_____

_____

_____

_____

A Moment with Max

Max shares these insights with us in his book *The Applause of Heaven.*

The Message is clear. As long as Jesus is one of many options, he is no option. As long as you can carry your burdens alone, you don't need a burden bearer. As long as your situation brings you no grief, you will receive no comfort. And as long as you can take him or leave him, you might as well leave him, because he won't be taken half-heartedly.

But when you mourn, when you get to the point of sorrow for your sins, when you admit that you have no other option but to cast all your cares on him, and when there is truly no other name that you can call, then cast all your cares on him, for he is waiting in the midst of the storm.

2. What prevents us from feeling deep sorrow and remorse for our sins?

_____

_____

_____

_____

_____

_____

3. Explain how a sinless God can receive us as sinful people.

_____

_____

_____

_____

_____

_____

_____

A Message from the Word

God, be merciful to me
    because you are loving.
    Because you are always ready to be merciful,
      wipe out all my wrongs.
² Wash away all my guilt
    and make me clean again.
³ I know about my wrongs,
    and I can't forget my sin.
⁴ You are the only one I have sinned against;
    I have done what you say is wrong.
    You are right when you speak
      and fair when you judge.
⁵ I was brought into this world in sin.
    In sin my mother gave birth to me.
⁶ You want me to be completely truthful,
    so teach me wisdom.
⁷ Take away my sin, and I will be clean.
    Wash me, and I will be whiter than snow.
⁸ Make me hear sounds of joy and gladness;
    let the bones you crushed be happy again.
⁹ Turn your face from my sins
    and wipe out all my guilt.
¹⁰ Create in me a pure heart, God,
    and make my spirit right again.

Psalm 51:1-10

33

4. What would it feel like to have your weakest and darkest actions exposed?

_____

_____

_____

_____

_____

5. What does this psalm teach us about true repentance?

_____

_____

_____

_____

_____

6. What do you think it means to God to see us grieve over our sins?

_____

_____

_____

_____

_____

_____

_____

More from the Word

Happy is the person
    whose sins are forgiven,
   whose wrongs are pardoned.
² Happy is the person
    whom the Lord does not consider guilty
      and in whom there is nothing false.
³ When I kept things to myself,

I felt weak deep inside me.
    I moaned all day long.
4 Day and night you punished me.
    My strength was gone as in the summer heat.
5 Then I confessed my sins to you
    and didn't hide my guilt.
I said, "I will confess my sins to the Lord,"
    and you forgave my guilt.

Psalm 32:1–5

7. How does unconfessed sin eat away at a person?

_____

_____

_____

_____

_____ 35

_____

_____

_____

8. In what ways do we deceive ourselves about the reality or consequences of our sins?

_____

_____

_____

_____

_____

_____

9. How does God lead us to repentance?

_____

_____

_____

_____

_____

_____

My Reflections

"A prison of pride is filled with self-made men and women determined to pull themselves up by their own bootstraps, even if they land on their rear ends. It doesn't matter what they did or to whom they did it or where they will end up; it only matters that 'I did it my way.'" —Max

Journal

How can I demonstrate my gratitude to God for his forgiveness?

_____

_____

_____

_____

37

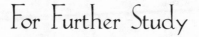

For Further Study

To study more about our struggle with sin, read Isaiah 30:15; Romans 6:11-18; 7:14-25.

Additional Questions

10. How can we sometimes sin and not be bothered by it?

_____

_____

_____

_____

_____

_____

_____

11. Describe what we lose when we sin.

_____

_____

_____

_____

_____

_____

12. Explain the balance between grieving over our sin and fully accepting God's forgiveness and freedom.

_____

_____

_____

_____

_____

_____

Additional Thoughts

_____

_____

_____

_____

_____

_____

_____

_____

_____

_____

_____

_____

The Glorious Ordinary

"The angel came in the night because that is when lights are best seen and that is when they are most needed. God comes into the common for the same reason. His most powerful tools are the simplest." —Max Lucado

1. What is meekness? Describe someone you know who has this quality.

_____

_____

_____

_____

_____

_____

_____

_____

_____

A Moment with Max

Max shares these insights with us in his book *The Applause of Heaven*.

That's why the announcement [of Jesus' birth] went first to the shepherds. They didn't ask God if he was sure he knew what he was doing. Had the angel gone to the theologians, they would have first consulted their commentaries. Had he gone to the elite, they would have looked around to see if anyone was watching. Had he gone to the successful, they would have first looked at their calendars.

So he went to the shepherds. Men who didn't have a reputation to protect or an ax to grind or a ladder to climb. Men who didn't know enough to tell God that angels don't sing to sheep and that messiahs aren't found wrapped in rags and sleeping in a feed trough.

So...
while the theologians were sleeping
and the elite were dreaming
and the successful were snoring,
the meek were kneeling.

They were kneeling before the One only the meek will see. They were kneeling in front of Jesus.

42

2. What things keep people from recognizing and worshiping Jesus as the Messiah?

_____

_____

_____

_____

_____

3. Why is it difficult for most of us to develop and display meekness?

_____

_____

_____

_____

_____

_____

A Message from the Word

²⁶ Brothers and sisters, look at what you were when God called you. Not many of you were wise in the way the world judges wisdom. Not many of you had great influence. Not many of you came from important families. ²⁷ But God chose the foolish things of the world to shame the wise, and he chose the weak things of the world to shame the strong. ²⁸ He chose what the world thinks is unimportant and what the world looks down on and thinks is nothing in order to destroy what the world thinks is important. ²⁹ God did this so that no one can brag in his presence. ³⁰ Because of God you are in Christ Jesus, who has become for us wisdom from God. In Christ we are put right with God, and have been made holy, and have been set free from sin. ³¹ So, as the Scripture says, "If someone wants to brag, he should brag only about the Lord."

1 Corinthians 1:26–31

43

4. What makes one person see himself as better than another?

_____

_____

_____

_____

_____

5. List some reasons why God chooses to use the meek rather than the proud to accomplish his purposes.

_____

_____

_____

_____

_____

6. How does God's choice to use the meek go against the values of our culture?

_____

_____

_____

_____

_____

44

More from the Word

[20] With God's power working in us, God can do much, much more than anything we can ask or imagine. [21] To him be glory in the church and in Christ Jesus for all time, forever and ever. Amen.

[1] I am in prison because I belong to the Lord. God chose you to be his people, so I urge you now to live the life to which God called you. [2] Always be humble, gentle, and patient, accepting each other in love. [3] You are joined together with peace through the Spirit, so make every effort to continue together in this way. [4] There is one body and one Spirit, and God called you to have one hope. [5] There is one Lord, one faith, and one baptism. [6] There is one God and Father of everything. He rules everything and is everywhere and is in everything.

Ephesians 3:20—4:6

7. How can a meek spirit allow God's power to shine brighter?

_____

_____

_____

_____

_____

_____

8. What is the opposite of meekness?

_____

_____

_____

_____ 45

_____

_____

9. How can humility bind believers together?

_____

_____

_____

_____

_____

_____

My Reflections

"A small cathedral outside Bethlehem marks the supposed birthplace of Jesus. Behind a high altar in the church is a cave, a little cavern lit by silver lamps. You can enter the main edifice and admire the ancient church. You can also enter the quiet cave where a star embedded in the floor recognizes the birth of the King. There is one stipulation, however. You have to stoop. The door is so low you can't go in standing up.

"The same is true of the Christ. You can see the world standing tall, but to witness the Savior, you have to get on your knees." —Max

Journal

What steps can I take to cultivate a meek spirit?

_____

_____

_____

_____

_____

_____

_____

_____

_____

_____

For Further Study

To study more about meekness, read Psalm 25:8-9; 37:5-11; Luke 14:7-11; 1 Peter 3:1-4; 5:6-9.

Additional Questions

10. Explain why you think God values meekness.

_____

_____

_____

_____

_____

_____

_____

11. In what ways does it take strength to be meek?

_____

_____

_____

_____

_____

_____

12. Compare meekness and humility.

_____

_____

_____

_____

_____

_____

Additional Thoughts

_____

_____

49

_____

_____

_____

_____

_____

_____

_____

_____

_____

_____

_____

_____

The Satisfied Thirst

"If anyone is thirsty,' Jesus once said, 'let him come to me and drink.'" —Max Lucado

1. What things do people falsely assume will quench their spiritual thirst?

_____

_____

_____

_____

_____

_____

_____

_____

A Moment with Max

Max shares these insights with us in his book *The Applause of Heaven*.

Some would rather die than admit it. Others admit it and escape death.

"God, I need help."

So the thirsty come. A ragged lot we are, bound together by broken dreams and collapsed promises. Fortunes that were never made. Families that were never built. Promises that were never kept. Wide-eyed children trapped in the basement of our own failures.

And we are very thirsty.

Not thirsty for fame, possessions, passion, or romance. We've drunk from those pools. They are salt water in the desert. They don't quench—they kill.

"Blessed are those who hunger and thirst for righteousness . . ."

Righteousness. That's it. That's what we are thirsty for. We're thirsty for a clean conscience. We crave a clean slate. We yearn for a fresh start. We pray for a hand that will enter the dark cavern of our world and do for us the one thing we can't do for ourselves—make us right again.

2. Do you believe everyone craves a clear conscience? Explain your answer.

52

_____

_____

_____

_____

_____

_____

3. Explain how a clean conscience brings peace and fulfillment.

_____

_____

_____

_____

_____

A Message from the Word

[9] Jesus told this story to some people who thought they were very good and looked down on everyone else: [10] "A Pharisee and a tax collector both went to the Temple to pray. [11] The Pharisee stood alone and prayed, 'God, I thank you that I am not like other people who steal, cheat, or take part in adultery, or even like this tax collector. [12] I give up eating twice a week, and I give one-tenth of everything I get!'

[13] "The tax collector, standing at a distance, would not even look up to heaven. But he beat on his chest because he was so sad. He said, 'God, have mercy on me, a sinner.' [14] I tell you, when this man went home, he was right with God, but the Pharisee was not. All who make themselves great will be made humble, but all who make themselves humble will be made great."

Luke 18:9-14

4. According to this story, how can a person be right with God?

_____

_____

_____

_____

_____

5. What kind of righteousness does God offer to us?

_____

_____

_____

_____

_____

6. What stands in the way of our receiving the righteousness God desires?

_____

_____

_____

_____

_____

More from the Word

[7] Those things were important to me, but now I think they are worth nothing because of Christ. [8] Not only those things, but I think that all things are worth nothing compared with the greatness of knowing Christ Jesus my Lord. Because of him, I have lost all those things, and now I know they are worthless trash. This allows me to have Christ [9] and to belong to him. Now I am right with God, not because I followed the law, but because I believed in Christ. God uses my faith to make me right with him. [10] I want to know Christ and the power that raised him from the dead. I want to share in his sufferings and become like him in his death.

Philippians 3:7-10

7. How can you determine a person's priorities and values?

_____

_____

_____

_____

_____

8. How does the fact that we belong to God change the way we view ourselves and our possessions?

_____

_____

_____

_____

_____

9. Describe in your own words what it means to know Christ.

_____

_____

_____

_____

_____

My Reflections

"We usually get what we hunger and thirst for. The problem is, the treasures
of earth don't satisfy. The promise is, the treasures of heaven do.

"Blessed are those, then, who hold their earthly possessions in open
palms. Blessed are those who, if everything they own were taken from
them, would be, at most, inconvenienced, because their true wealth is else-
where. Blessed are those who are totally dependent upon Jesus for their
joy.'"   —Max

Journal

In what practical way can I seek God's righteousness?

_____

_____

_____

_____

_____

_____

_____

_____

_____

_____

_____

_____

_____

_____

_____

_____

_____

For Further Study

To study more about seeking God and his righteousness, read Psalm 42:1-3; 73:21-28; Jeremiah 29:11-13; Ephesians 3:16-19.

Additional Questions

10. What is the difference between *wanting* something and *craving* something?

_____

_____

_____

_____

_____

_____

_____

11. How would we live differently if we hungered for God like we crave our favorite foods?

_____

_____

_____

_____

_____

_____

12. How does righteousness satisfy us like food and water satisfiy our hunger and thirst?

_____

_____

_____

_____

_____

_____

Additional Thoughts

_____

_____

59

_____

_____

_____

_____

_____

_____

_____

_____

_____

_____

The Power of Mercy

"The worst part of all is that, without forgiveness, bitterness is all that is left."

—Max Lucado

61

1. Complete this statement: A picture of mercy is a person who . . .

_____

_____

_____

_____

_____

_____

_____

_____

A Moment with Max

Max shares these insights with us in his book *The Applause of Heaven*.

Do you have a hole in your heart?

Perhaps the wound is old . . . and you're angry.

Or perhaps the wound is fresh . . . and you're hurt.

Part of you is broken, and the other part is bitter. Part of you wants to cry, and part of you wants to fight. The tears you cry are hot because they come from your heart, and there is a fire burning in your heart. It's the fire of anger. It's blazing. It's consuming. Its flames leap up under a steaming pot of revenge.

And you are left with a decision: "Do I put the fire out or heat it up? Do I get over it or get even? Do I release it or resent it? Do I let my hurts heal, or do I let hurt turn into hate?"

2. Describe the struggle between releasing or resenting someone after they've hurt you.

_____

_____

62

_____

_____

_____

_____

3. Explain how it benefits us to show mercy to others.

_____

_____

_____

_____

_____

A Message from the Word

²³ "The kingdom of heaven is like a king who decided to collect the money his servants owed him. ²⁴ When the king began to collect his money, a servant who owed him several million dollars was brought to him. ²⁵ But the servant did not have enough money to pay his master, the king. So the master ordered that everything the servant owned should be sold, even the servant's wife and children. Then the money would be used to pay the king what the servant owed.

²⁶ "But the servant fell on his knees and begged, 'Be patient with me, and I will pay you everything I owe.' ²⁷ The master felt sorry for his servant and told him he did not have to pay it back. Then he let the servant go free.

²⁸ "Later, that same servant found another servant who owed him a few dollars. The servant grabbed him around the neck and said, 'Pay me the money you owe me!'

²⁹ "The other servant fell on his knees and begged him, 'Be patient with me, and I will pay you everything I owe.'

³⁰ "But the first servant refused to be patient. He threw the other servant into prison until he could pay everything he owed. ³¹ When the other servants saw what had happened, they were very sorry. So they went and told their master all that had happened.

³² "Then the master called his servant in and said, 'You evil servant! Because you begged me to forget what you owed, I told you that you did not have to pay anything. ³³ You should have showed mercy to that other servant, just as I showed mercy to you.' ³⁴ The master was very angry and put the servant in prison to be punished until he could pay everything he owed.

³⁵ "This king did what my heavenly Father will do to you if you do not forgive your brother or sister from your heart."

Matthew 18:23–35

63

4. In light of this parable, how important would you say it is for us to be merciful?

_____

_____

_____

_____

5. Why do you think God puts such a priority on our willingness to show mercy?

_____

_____

_____

_____

_____

6. How should God's mercy to us impact the way we treat others?

_____

_____

_____

_____

_____

More from the Word

[12] In everything you say and do, remember that you will be judged by the law that makes people free. [13] So you must show mercy to others, or God will not show mercy to you when he judges you. But the person who shows mercy can stand without fear at the judgment.

James 2:12–13

7. Which is more powerful: judgment or mercy? Why?

_____

_____

_____

_____

_____

8. In your own words, define judgment without mercy.

_____

_____

_____

_____

_____

9. What most often stands in the way of our showing mercy?

_____

_____

_____

_____

_____

My Reflections

"Are you allowing your hurts to turn into hates? If so, ask yourself: Is it working? Has your hatred done you any good? Has your resentment brought you any relief, any peace? Has it granted you any joy?

"Allow the hole in your heart to heal.' " —Max

Journal

To whom do I need to show mercy? How?

For Further Study

To study more about mercy, read Matthew 6:14-15; Luke 6:32-38; Romans 11:30-32; 1 Timothy 1:15-17; Jude 1:22-23.

Additional Questions

10. Describe an act of mercy you have witnessed or experienced.

_____

_____

_____

_____

_____

_____

_____

11. What does showing mercy bring into our lives?

_____

_____

_____

_____

_____

_____

_____

12. Explain how mercy is different from forgiveness.

_____

_____

_____

_____

_____

_____

_____

Additional Thoughts

_____

_____

_____

_____

_____

_____

_____

_____

_____

_____

_____

_____

_____

The Guarded Heart

"Note the order of this beatitude: first, purify the heart, then you will see God ... You change your life by changing your heart."

—Max Lucado

1. Describe some ways in which our current culture does or does not value purity.

_____

_____

_____

_____

_____

_____

_____

_____

_____

A Moment with Max

Max shares these insights with us in his book *The Applause of Heaven*.

To Jesus' listeners, the heart was the totality of the inner person—the control tower, the cockpit. The heart was thought of as the seat of the character—the origin of desires, affections, perceptions, thoughts, reasoning, imagination, conscience, intentions, purpose, will, and faith.

Thus a proverb admonished, "Above all else, guard your heart, for it is the wellspring of life."

To the Hebrew mind, the heart is a freeway cloverleaf where all emotions and prejudices and wisdom converge. It is a switch house that receives freight cars loaded with moods, ideas, emotions, and convictions and puts them on the right track.

And just as a low-grade oil or alloyed gasoline would cause you to question the performance of a refinery, evil acts and impure thoughts cause us to question the condition of our hearts.

2. Describe in your own words what it means to guard your heart.

_____

72

_____

_____

_____

_____

_____

3. In what practical ways can we guard our hearts from evil?

_____

_____

_____

_____

_____

_____

A Message from the Word

⁵ Let everyone see that you are gentle and kind. The Lord is coming soon. ⁶ Do not worry about anything, but pray and ask God for everything you need, always giving thanks. ⁷ And God's peace, which is so great we cannot understand it, will keep your hearts and minds in Christ Jesus.

⁸ Brothers and sisters, think about the things that are good and worthy of praise. Think about the things that are true and honorable and right and pure and beautiful and respected. ⁹ Do what you learned and received from me, what I told you, and what you saw me do. And the God who gives peace will be with you.

Philippians 4:5-9

4. Why is it so difficult to discipline our thoughts?

_____

_____

_____

_____

_____

_____

5. How do our thoughts affect the state of our hearts?

_____

_____

_____

_____

_____

_____

6. What actions must we take before we can expect God's peace to guard our hearts?

_____

_____

_____

_____

_____

More from the Word

74 ²³ Be careful what you think,
    because your thoughts run your life.
²⁴ Don't use your mouth to tell lies;
    don't ever say things that are not true.
²⁵ Keep your eyes focused on what is right,
    and look straight ahead to what is good.
²⁶ Be careful what you do,
    and always do what is right.
²⁷ Don't turn off the road of goodness;
    keep away from evil paths.

Proverbs 4:23-27

7. How would you describe to a child the best way to stay out of trouble?

_____

_____

_____

_____

8. Why is it so important to keep our eyes focused on what is good and true?

_____

_____

_____

_____

_____

_____

9. List some things that distract us from doing what is right.

_____

_____

_____

_____

_____

_____

_____

My Reflections

"The state of your heart dictates whether you harbor a grudge or give grace, seek self-pity or seek Christ, drink human misery or taste God's mercy. No wonder, then, the wise man begs, 'Above all else, guard your heart.'"
—Max

Journal

What are the biggest threats to the purity of my heart right now?

_____

_____

_____

_____

_____

_____

_____

_____

_____

_____

_____

_____

_____

_____

_____

For Further Study

To study more about guarding your heart, read Matthew 15:17-20; Psalm 24:3-5; 86:11-13; Proverbs 20:9

Additional Questions

10. What is your first thought when you think of purity?

_____

_____

_____

_____

_____

_____

_____

11. What simple steps can we take to avoid impurity?

_____

_____

_____

_____

_____

_____

_____

12. Why is accountability crucial in our quest for purity?

_____

_____

_____

_____

_____

_____

Additional Thoughts

_____

_____

_____

_____

_____

_____

_____

_____

_____

_____

_____

_____

_____

The Seed of Peace

"Sowing seeds of peace is like sowing beans. You don't know why it works; you just know it does." —Max Lucado

1. How do you and your family members work to maintain harmony in your home?

_____

_____

_____

_____

_____

_____

_____

_____

A Moment with Max

Max shares these insights with us in his book *The Applause of Heaven*.

Want to see a miracle? Try this.

Take a seed the size of a freckle. Put it under several inches of dirt. Give it enough water, light, and fertilizer. And get ready. A mountain will be moved. It doesn't matter that the ground is a zillion times the weight of the seed. The seed will push it back.

Every spring, dreamers around the world plant tiny hopes in overturned soil. And every spring, their hopes press against impossible odds and blossom.

Never underestimate the power of a seed.

As far as I know, James, the epistle writer, wasn't a farmer, but he knew the power of a seed sown in fertile soil.

"Those who are peacemakers will plant seeds of peace and reap a harvest of goodness."

The principle for peace is the same as the principle for crops: Never underestimate the power of a seed.

2. How does peace work like a seed?

_____

_____

_____

_____

_____

3. If peace works like a seed, whose job is it to plant it? How?

_____

_____

_____

_____

_____

A Message from the Word

[17] But the wisdom that comes from God is first of all pure, then peaceful, gentle, and easy to please. This wisdom is always ready to help those who are troubled and to do good for others. It is always fair and honest. [18] People who work for peace in a peaceful way plant a good crop of right-living.

[1] Do you know where your fights and arguments come from? They come from the selfish desires that war within you. [2] You want things, but you do not have them. So you are ready to kill and are jealous of other people, but you still cannot get what you want. So you argue and fight. You do not get what you want, because you do not ask God. [3] Or when you ask, you do not receive because the reason you ask is wrong. You want things so you can use them for your own pleasures.

James 3:17—4:3

4. What is the quickest way to erode peace between friends?

_____

_____

_____

_____

_____

_____

5. Once an argument has started, why is it so difficult to stop?

_____

_____

_____

_____

_____

6. What things destroy your inner peace?

_____

_____

_____

_____

_____

More from the Word

[14] Wish good for those who harm you; wish them well and do not curse them. [15] Be happy with those who are happy, and be sad with those who are sad. [16] Live in peace with each other. Do not be proud, but make friends with those who seem unimportant. Do not think how smart you are.

[17] If someone does wrong to you, do not pay him back by doing wrong to him. Try to do what everyone thinks is right. [18] Do your best to live in peace with everyone. [19] My friends, do not try to punish others when they wrong you, but wait for God to punish them with his anger. It is written: "I will punish those who do wrong; I will repay them," says the Lord.

Romans 12:14-19

7. What part does pride play in creating disunity?

_____

_____

_____

_____

_____

8. How does giving up our desire for vengeance help us plant peace?

_____

_____

_____

_____

_____

_____

9. What sense of responsibility do you feel for living peaceably with the people around you?

_____

_____

_____

_____

_____

_____

My Reflections

"How good are you at sowing seeds of peace?

"Pause for a moment and think about the people who make up your world. Take a stroll through the gallery of faces that are significant to you.

"Want to see a miracle? Plant a word of love heartdeep in a person's life. Nurture it with a smile and a prayer, and watch what happens . . . Never underestimate the power of a seed." —Max

Journal

In what relationship can I plant seeds of peace today? How?

For Further Study

To study more about living in peace, read Psalm 34:11-14; 37:37; Romans 14:16-19; Galatians 5:22-23; 1 Thessalonians 5:12-15; Titus 3:1-2; Hebrews 12:14-15.

Additional Questions

10. In what kinds of life situations is it most difficult to sow peace?

_____

_____

_____

_____

_____

_____

_____

11. What does a person's aptitude for sowing peace reveal about his or her relationship with Jesus Christ?

_____

_____

_____

_____

_____

_____

12. How does your life function differently when you are living at peace with others?

_____

_____

_____

_____

_____

_____

Additional Thoughts

_____

_____

_____

_____

_____

_____

_____

_____

_____

_____

_____

_____

The Difficult Questions

"If God is so good, why do I hurt so bad?"
—Max Lucado

1. Why do you think God gave us free will?

_____

_____

_____

_____

_____

_____

_____

_____

_____

A Moment with Max

Max shares these insights with us in his book *The Applause of Heaven*.

Though the circumstances have [changed], the questions haven't. They are asked anytime the faithful suffer the consequences of the faithless. Anytime a person takes a step in the right direction, only to have her feet knocked out from under her, anytime a person does a good deed but suffers evil results, anytime a person takes a stand, only to end up flat on his face . . . the questions fall like rain.

"If God is really there, why am I here?"

"What did I do to deserve this?"

"Why are the righteous persecuted?"

Does God sometimes sit on his hands? Does God sometimes choose to do nothing? Does God sometimes opt for silence even when I'm screaming my loudest?

2. How would you answer the question, "Why is life so unfair?"

_____

_____

_____

_____

_____

_____

3. What helps you keep going when life is unfair?

_____

_____

_____

_____

_____

_____

A Message from the Word

[1] Since we have been made right with God by our faith, we have peace with God. This happened through our Lord Jesus Christ, [2] who has brought us into that blessing of God's grace that we now enjoy. And we are happy because of the hope we have of sharing God's glory. [3] We also have joy with our troubles, because we know that these troubles produce patience. [4] And patience produces character, and character produces hope. [5] And this hope will never disappoint us, because God has poured out his love to fill our hearts. He gave us his love through the Holy Spirit, whom God has given to us.

[6] When we were unable to help ourselves, at the moment of our need, Christ died for us, although we were living against God. [7] Very few people will die to save the life of someone else. Although perhaps for a good person someone might possibly die. [8] But God shows his great love for us in this way: Christ died for us while we were still sinners.

Romans 5:1-8

93

4. Explain in your own words how character produces hope.

_____

_____

_____

_____

_____

5. What unfair treatment did Christ endure? Why?

_____

_____

_____

_____

_____

6. How can Christ's example help us endure unfair hardships?

_____

_____

_____

_____

_____

More from the Word

[1] We have around us many people whose lives tell us what faith means. So let us run the race that is before us and never give up. We should remove from our lives anything that would get in the way and the sin that so easily holds us back. [2] Let us look only to Jesus, the One who began our faith and who makes it perfect. He suffered death on the cross. But he accepted the shame as if it were nothing because of the joy that God put before him. And now he is sitting at the right side of God's throne. [3] Think about Jesus' example. He held on while wicked people were doing evil things to him. So do not get tired and stop trying.

Hebrews 12:1-3

7. What was the goal Christ had in mind that helped him endure his suffering?

_____

_____

_____

_____

_____

_____

8. What kind of mindset can help carry us through life's difficulties?

_____

_____

_____

_____

_____

9. Why does God allow the godly to suffer?

_____

_____

_____

_____

_____

_____

My Reflections

"If you've asked for a mate, but you are still sleeping alone ... if you've asked for a child, but your womb stays barren ... if you've asked for healing, but are still hurting ...don't think God isn't listening. He is. And he is answering requests you are not even making." —Max

Journal

What needs should I trust God to meet according to his will, not my own?

For Further Study

To study more about perseverance in difficult times, read Matthew 5:10–11; 2 Timothy 2:1–3; 4:5; James 1:2–4, 12–15; 5:10–11; 1 Peter 2:18–25.

Additional Questions

10. Respond to this statement: I must be doing something right, if this many people are against it.

_____

_____

_____

_____

_____

_____

11. Describe the feelings associated with being falsely accused.

_____

_____

_____

_____

_____

_____

12. To what kind of people is righteousness a threat? Why?

_____

_____

_____

_____

_____

Additional Thoughts

_____

_____

99

_____

_____

_____

_____

_____

_____

_____

_____

_____

_____

_____

_____

The Applause of Heaven

"When you think of a world where there will be no reason to cry, ever, doesn't it make you want to go home?" —Max Lucado

1. Think of the safest place you have ever known. What made you feel safe there?

_____

_____

_____

_____

_____

_____

_____

_____

A Moment with Max

Max shares these insights with us in his book *The Applause of Heaven*.

You may not have noticed it, but you are closer to home than ever before. Each moment is a step taken. Each breath is a page turned. Each day is a mile marked, a mountain climbed. You are closer to home than you've ever been.

Before you know it, your appointed arrival time will come; you'll descend the ramp and enter the city.

You'll see faces that are waiting for you. You'll hear your name spoken by those who love you. And, maybe, just maybe—in the back, behind the crowds—the One who would rather die than live without you will remove his pierced hands from his heavenly robe and . . . applaud.

2. What do you imagine you will enjoy most about heaven?

_____

_____

_____

_____

_____

_____

3. What do you hope God says to you when you stand before him in heaven for the first time?

_____

_____

_____

_____

_____

_____

A Message from the Word

¹ We know that our body—the tent we live in here on earth—will be destroyed. But when that happens, God will have a house for us. It will not be a house made by human hands; instead, it will be a home in heaven that will last forever. ² But now we groan in this tent. We want God to give us our heavenly home, ³ because it will clothe us so we will not be naked. ⁴ While we live in this body, we have burdens, and we groan. We do not want to be naked, but we want to be clothed with our heavenly home. Then this body that dies will be fully covered with life. ⁵ This is what God made us for, and he has given us the Spirit to be a guarantee for this new life.

⁶ So we always have courage. We know that while we live in this body, we are away from the Lord. ⁷ We live by what we believe, not by what we can see. ⁸ So I say that we have courage. We really want to be away from this body and be at home with the Lord. ⁹ Our only goal is to please God whether we live here or there, ¹⁰ because we must all stand before Christ to be judged. Each of us will receive what we should get—good or bad—for the things we did in the earthly body.

2 Corinthians 5:1-10

4. What gives us courage to live for Christ in this life?   *103*

_____

_____

_____

_____

_____

_____

5. Describe the difference between living by what we *believe* and living by what we can *see*.

_____

_____

_____

6. What would be the most meaningful reward you could receive in heaven?

_____

_____

_____

_____

_____

More from the Word

[11] In Christ we were chosen to be God's people, because from the very beginning God had decided this in keeping with his plan. And he is the One who makes everything agree with what he decides and wants. [12] We are the first people who hoped in Christ, and we were chosen so that we would bring praise to God's glory. [13] So it is with you. When you heard the true teaching—the Good News about your salvation—you believed in Christ. And in Christ, God put his special mark of ownership on you by giving you the Holy Spirit that he had promised. [14] That Holy Spirit is the guarantee that we will receive what God promised for his people until God gives full freedom to those who are his—to bring praise to God's glory.

Ephesians 1:11-14

7. How does it make you feel to know that God chose you to be his child?

_____

_____

_____

_____

_____

_____

_____

8. What is our inheritance as children of God?

_____

_____

_____

_____

_____

_____ *105*

_____

9. When you make the difficult choices to obey God, what makes it worthwhile for you?

_____

_____

_____

_____

_____

_____

My Reflections

"Faces of home.

"That is what makes the promise at the end of the Beatitudes so compelling: 'Rejoice and be glad, because great is your reward in heaven.'

"What is our reward? Home." —Max

Journal

How can I show my gratitude to God for the promise of eternal life?

For Further Study

To study more about the rewards of faith, read Proverbs 11:18; 12:14; 14:14; 19:17; Jeremiah 17:9–10; Matthew 5:11–12; 6:4; 10:40–42; Luke 6:31–36; Hebrews 11:6, 24–26.

Additional Questions

10. What fears and uncertainties do you have about the afterlife?

_____

_____

_____

_____

_____

11. How can you be sure you will go to heaven?

_____

_____

_____

_____

_____

12. What hinders people from accepting the gift of eternal life?

_____

_____

_____

_____

_____

_____

Additional Thoughts

_____

_____

109

_____

_____

_____

_____

_____

_____

_____

_____

_____

_____

_____

The Whole Blessed Picture

"How do you change your heart? Jesus gave the plan on the mountain." —Max Lucado

1. Why is it difficult for most people to make lasting changes in their lives?

_____

_____

_____

_____

_____

_____

_____

_____

A Moment with Max

Max shares these insights with us in his book *The Applause of Heaven*.

Matthew 5 describes God's radical reconstruction of the heart.

Observe the sequence. First, we recognize we are in need (we're poor in spirit). Next, we repent of our self-sufficiency (we mourn). We quit calling the shots and surrender control to God (we're meek). So grateful are we for his presence that we yearn for more of him (we hunger and thirst). As we grow closer to him, we become more like him. We forgive others (we're merciful). We change our outlook (We're pure in heart). We love others (we're peacemakers). We endure injustice (we're persecuted).

It's no casual shift of attitude. It is a demolition of the old structure and a creation of the new. The more radical the change, the greater the joy. And it's worth every effort, for this is the joy of God.

2. If we say we trust God, then why do we hesitate to allow him to change our hearts?

_____

_____

_____

_____

_____

_____

3. Describe the methods God uses to reconstruct a person's heart.

_____

_____

_____

_____

_____

_____

A Message from the Word

[16] From this time on we do not think of anyone as the world does. In the past we thought of Christ as the world thinks, but we no longer think of him in that way. [17] If anyone belongs to Christ, there is a new creation. The old things have gone; everything is made new! [18] All this is from God. Through Christ, God made peace between us and himself, and God gave us the work of telling everyone about the peace we can have with him. [19] God was in Christ, making peace between the world and himself. In Christ, God did not hold the world guilty of its sins. And he gave us this message of peace. [20] So we have been sent to speak for Christ. It is as if God is calling to you through us. We speak for Christ when we beg you to be at peace with God. [21] Christ had no sin, but God made him become sin so that in Christ we could become right with God.

[1] We are workers together with God, so we beg you: Do not let the grace that you received from God be for nothing.

2 Corinthians 5:16—6:1

4. What is the worldly way of thinking about Christ?

_____

_____

_____

_____

_____

_____

5. In what ways are you a new creation in Jesus Christ?

_____

_____

_____

_____

_____

_____

6. Describe what it means to let the grace of God be for nothing.

_____

_____

_____

_____

_____

More from the Word

[1] At that time the followers came to Jesus and asked, "Who is greatest in the kingdom of heaven?"

[2] Jesus called a little child to him and stood the child before his followers. [3] Then he said, "I tell you the truth, you must change and become like little children. Otherwise, you will never enter the kingdom of heaven. [4] The greatest person in the kingdom of heaven is the one who makes himself humble like this child.

Matthew 18:1-4

7. How do children love, trust, and learn differently than adults?

_____

_____

_____

_____

_____

_____

8. In what specific ways should we strive to become more like little children?

_____

_____

_____

_____

_____

_____

9. What childlike characteristics would you like to cultivate in your own life?

_____

_____

_____

_____

_____

_____

My Reflections

"And though your heart isn't perfect, it isn't rotten. And though you aren't invincible, at least you're plugged in. And you can bet that he who made you knows just how to purify you—from the inside out." —Max

Journal

What area of my life do I need to surrender to God's transforming work?

For Further Study

To study more about how God changes us, read Psalm 86:11–13;
Luke 5:36–39; Romans 10:9–10; 12:1–2.

Additional Questions

10. Describe the difference between changing from the *inside out* and
changing from the *outside in*.

_____

_____

_____

_____

_____

11. List some ways we can change bad habits.

_____

_____

_____

_____

_____

_____

12. How can we be more receptive to God's changing work in our hearts?

_____

_____

_____

_____

_____

Additional Thoughts

_____

_____

_____

_____

_____

_____

_____

_____

_____

_____

_____

_____

_____